P9-DBL-736

**COLORADO
MOUNTAIN CLUB
PACK GUIDE**

ROCKY
MOUNTAIN
Wildflowers

MARLENE BORNEMAN

and

JAMES ELLS

The Colorado Mountain Club Press
Golden, Colorado

Rocky Mountain Wildflowers
© 2012 by The Colorado Mountain Club

All rights reserved. No part of this publication may be reproduced or transmitted in any form or by any means, electronic or mechanical, including photocopying, recording, or by any information storage and retrieval system without permission in writing from the publisher.

PUBLISHED BY

The Colorado Mountain Club Press
710 Tenth Street, Suite 200, Golden, Colorado 80401
303-996-2743   e-mail: cmcpress@cmc.org

Founded in 1912, The Colorado Mountain Club is the largest outdoor recreation, education, and conservation organization in the Rocky Mountains. Look for our books at your local bookstore or outdoor retailer or online at www.cmc.org/books.

CONTACTING THE PUBLISHER
We would appreciate it if readers would alert us to any errors or outdated information by contacting us at the address above.

DISTRIBUTED TO THE BOOK TRADE BY
The Mountaineers Books, 1001 SW Klickitat Way, Suite 201, Seattle, WA 98134, 800-553-4453, www.mountaineersbooks.org

COVER PHOTO: Todd Caudle, skylinepress.com.

We gratefully acknowledge the financial support of the people of Colorado through the Scientific and Cultural Facilities District of greater metropolitan Denver for our publishing activities.

First Edition

ISBN 978-1-937052-03-4

Printed in China

CONTENTS

YELLOW WILDFLOWERS

BLUE WILDFLOWERS

Seeing Wildflowers

SUSAN J. TWEIT

*Nobody sees a flower—really—it is
so small—we haven't time—and to
see takes time…*

—Georgia O'Keeffe

I t's pretty hard to miss Rocky Mountain wildflowers. Hundreds of species color the continent's highest and longest mountain chain from lower elevations where crocus-like sand lilies bloom in starry abundance to mountain meadows perfumed by lilac-blue Rocky Mountain iris, and wind-blasted alpine tundra dotted with pink moss campion and other ground-hugging "belly-flowers."

But to really see wildflowers in the sense painter Georgia O'Keeffe meant requires more than just an "Oh wow!" glance. Identifying the eye-catching blooms opens a door to an entire community of lives and relationships. Wildflowers are so much more than pretty scenery; their relationships and behavior weave the fabric of these majestic landscapes.

The flowers and their astonishing variety of forms—from straight-forward saucers and disks to bells, urns, funnels, tubes, stars, and even bulbous hoods and slippers—are designed for a very basic purpose. They are the siren songs of flowering plants, existing simply to facilitate sex and reproduction.

Plants are rooted in place; they can't chase potential partners. So they rely on proxies—pollinators—to transfer their genetic material from flower to flower. Plants expend a large portion of their energy to produce flowers in order to attract a partner to transfer the plant pollen—or sperm—to another flower's pistil, where it can fertilize the embryonic seeds.

The business of attracting a pollination partner is not delicate. In fact, most plants rely on bribery: they offer food in exchange for pollination by birds and insects.

Tubular red flowers like scarlet gilia, for example, appeal to hummingbirds. Because birds are attuned to red light wavelengths plants use red like a neon sign that screams: "Food! Here!"

A hummingbird works a patch of gilia with the focus of a famished diner, darting from blossom to blossom, thrusting its slender beak deep into each floral tube to reach the nectaries and slurping high-energy liquid with its brush-tipped tongue before zipping on.

As the hummer pushes its beak into the flower, its forehead brushes the sticky surface of the flower's pistil. Grains of pollen picked up at other flowers adhere to the pistil, bringing their particular set of genes to fertilize this flower. As the hummer backs away, it brushes the flower's stamens, picking up the pollen it will carry to another blossom.

The diminutive birds and the red tubular wildflowers have a tight relationship: the plants time their bloom to when their hovering—and hungry—pollinators arrive from winter homes hundreds of miles away in southern Mexico and Central America. The flowers depend on hummingbird pollination to ensure a good crop of young seeds just as the hummingbirds depend on the flowers' nectar to refuel and produce their own "crop" of young hummers.

Colorado blue columbines demonstrate another close relationship. Wherever bumblebees are their main pollinators, these plants produce flowers in a dark blue color easily visible to bees, as well as nectaries in short spurs the bees' tongues can reach. But where long-tongued sphinx moths are instead the primary pollinators, Colorado blue columbine flowers are pale blue—thus more visible in the low light of evening when sphinx moths fly—and sprout long-spurred nectaries to accommodate the longer tongue of the sphinx moth.

Bees, butterflies, and other insects are attuned to blue, yellow, and white light wavelengths, but not to red. Evolutionary biologists think that as flowers acquired color to stand out, their pollinators evolved color vision to spot them.

Wildflowers also use visual cues and scents to guide their pollinators. The yellow lines leading into the throats of Rocky Mountain penstemons and the dark purple lines on Rocky Mountain iris, for instance, serve as road signs guiding pollinators on a route that maximizes the chances of fertilization for these flowers.

Plants even tell pollinators when an individual flower has already been pollinated and thus quits producing food. The bright gold spot on the top petal of lupine flowers advertises fat-rich pollen to native bees. Once the flower has been fertilized the spot turns purple, like a "closed" sign.

Wildflower shapes are also tailored to pollinators. Flowers with narrow tubes appeal to long-tongued hummingbirds and moths, while fat tubes are designed to allow chubby-bodied bumblebees easy access. Flowers with open disks serve as landing platforms welcoming a variety of pollinators: butterflies, bees, seed-eating birds, beetles, and ants.

Evening primroses and other night-opening wildflowers avoid competing with the profusion of daytime wildflowers. Pale colors and disk-shaped flowers make them visible in moonlight. Persistent scents summon night-flying pollinators such as moths and bats.

Some less showy wildflowers enhance their attractiveness by offering pollinators warmth and nighttime shelter. Pasque flowers open their pale blossoms during sunny days when the parabolic disk-shaped blossoms focus the sun's warmth on the center of the flower. At night, the petals close, giving insects a cozy place to rest. Avalanche lilies manufacture compounds that generate enough heat to melt snow, attracting insects to their early-blooming flowers.

Of course, not all wildflowers play fair. The brightly colored and unusually shaped blossoms of calypso orchids only *appear* to offer food. Insects drawn into these trickster flowers pick up pollen in their fruitless search for nectar, pollinating the orchid blossoms for free.

Some pollinators don't play fair either. Small round holes chewed through the base of tubular wildflowers like gilia, penstemon, columbine, and evening primrose show where insects unable to reach deep into the flower have robbed the nectaries from outside, gaining a high-energy meal without providing pollination.

Pollination is only part of the wildflower story. Plants are this planet's food base, munched on by Rocky Mountain animals as different as grizzly bears, which sate post-hibernation hunger by digging up the starchy storage tubers of springbeauty from mountain meadows, and rabbit-like pikas, which harvest leaves and flowers from alpine grasslands for winter "hay."

Plants fight for their lives against these grazers by making a wide variety of chemical weapons, which render their flesh bad-tasting or even outright poisonous. Some of these compounds are used commercially as natural pesticides.

A few plants turn the tables and eat their consumers. Pinedrops grow in deep shade where they can't produce food from sunlight. They team with underground fungi for sugars and obtain crucial nitrogen by trapping insects in sticky droplets on their leafless stalks. Botanists call plants like pinedrops "protocarnivorous," or original carnivores.

Plants are equally clever about enlisting transportation to spread their seeds. The seeds of violets include an oil-rich handle attractive to foraging ants. An ant hauls the seeds back to her nest, eats the nutritious handle, and discards the uneaten seed to sprout. Other plants grow seeds with complicated prickles and hooks that snag in animal fur—or hikers' socks—and are carried long distances. That hook-and-fur design inspired the inventor of Velcro.

Plant–animal relationships weave the fabric of healthy Rocky Mountain landscapes. Unfortunately, these relationships are in peril from two growing factors: Invasive weeds such as field bindweed, yellow sweetclover, Dalmation toadflax, butter and eggs, and swamp verbena displace native plants, depriving pollinators and grazers of food; and global climate change severs plant–animal connections by shifting seasonal timing, so that, for instance, scarlet gilia could finish blooming before its hungry hummingbird pollinators arrive in migration. Understanding and restoring these relationships is something positive that humans can do to help.

Identifying Rocky Mountain wildflowers is the first step to "seeing" and honoring the complex and fascinating relationships that give the Rocky Mountains their enduring beauty. Use this guide to stop, look, learn—and enjoy!

ROCKY MOUNTAIN WILDFLOWERS

White Flowers

ALPINE PENNYCRESS
(WILD CANDYTUFT)
Noccaea montana (Thlaspi montanum)
Mustard family *Brassicaceae (Cruciferae)*

ECOLOGY: Foothills to alpine.

LOOK FOR slender stems topped with 1" balls
 of white flowers.

BLOOM: Spring–summer

ALPINE SPRINGBEAUTY
Claytonia megarhiza
Purslane family *Portulacaceae*

ECOLOGY: Alpine on scree.

LOOK FOR a small white
  flower and opposite, bright
  green, fleshy leaves.

BLOOM: Summer

13

AMERICAN BISTORT
Polygonum bistortoides
Buckwheat family *Polygonaceae*
ECOLOGY: Subalpine and alpine in moisture.
LOOK FOR a compact spike on a slender stalk.
BLOOM: Summer

AMERICAN (SPREADING) GLOBEFLOWER
Trollius laxus
Buttercup family *Ranunculaceae*

ECOLOGY: Montane to alpine.

LOOK FOR bright green, toothed foliage that distinguishes it from White Marigold *(Caltha leptosepala)*.

BLOOM: Spring–summer

BASTARD TOADFLAX
Comandra umbellata
Sandalwood family *Santalaceae*

ECOLOGY: Plains and foothills.

LOOK FOR a succulent plant with
  alternating, upright leaves and a domed,
  terminal umbel of white flowers.

BLOOM: Spring–early summer

BLADDER (WHITE) CAMPION
Silene latifolia (scouleri) alba
Pink family *Caryophyllaceae*
ECOLOGY: Plains to montane.
LOOK FOR inflated calyxes.
BLOOM: Summer–autumn

BRACTED (FERNLEAF) LOUSEWORT
Pedicularis bracteosa
Figwort family *Scrophulariaceae*

ECOLOGY: Montane to alpine in moist areas.

LOOK FOR pale yellow, ascending, beaked
  flowers in a terminal spike.

BLOOM: Summer

BROOK SAXIFRAGE
Saxifraga (Micranthes) odontoloma
Saxifrage family *Saxifragaceae*

ECOLOGY: Montane to alpine in wet places.

LOOK FOR glossy, toothed, basal leaves and white flowers.

BLOOM: Summer

19

BUCKBEAN
Menyanthes trifoliata
Buckbean family *Menyanthaceae*

ECOLOGY: Plains to montane in water.

LOOK FOR a white-flowered raceme
and upright, trifoliate leaves
growing in shallow water.

BLOOM: Summer

CANADIAN (MEADOW) ANEMONE
Anemone canadensis
Buttercup family *Ranunculaceae*

ECOLOGY: Plains to subalpine.

LOOK FOR saucer-shaped flowers with yellow,
brush-like centers subtended by a whorl of
deeply toothed leaves.

BLOOM: Spring–summer

CANADIAN WHITE VIOLET
Viola canadensis
Violet family *Violaceae*

ECOLOGY: Foothills to alpine in shade.

LOOK FOR patches of bright green
  leaves and white, bisymmetrical
  flowers in wet, shady areas.

BLOOM: Spring–midsummer

CLASPLEAF TWISTEDSTALK
Streptopus amplexifolius
Lily family *Liliaceae*

ECOLOGY: Foothills to subalpine in semishade and moisture.

LOOK FOR two-dimensional leaf arrangement and a flower at each node.

BLOOM: Summer

COLORADO FALSE HELLEBORE
Veratrum tenuipetalum
Lily family *Liliaceae*

ECOLOGY: Montane in open moist sites.

LOOK FOR a coarse, large plant with
parallel venation and a 4' stalk.

BLOOM: Summer

COMMON COWPARSNIP
Heracleum maximum (sphondylium)
Celery (Parsley) family *Apiaceae (Umbelliferae)*
ECOLOGY: Foothills to subalpine in wet places.
LOOK FOR a large, succulent plant on wet ground.
BLOOM: Summer

COMMON STARLILY (SANDLILY)
Leucocrinum montanum
Lily family *Liliaceae*

ECOLOGY: Plains and foothills among sagebrush.

LOOK FOR a tiny plant with six separated ̶w̶h̶i̶t̶e tepals (undifferentiated petals ̶a̶n̶d̶ sepals).

BLOOM: Spring–early summer

COMMON (TANSY) YARROW
Achillea millefolium (lanulosa)
Aster family *Asteraceae (Compositae)*
ECOLOGY: Foothills to alpine in dry areas.
LOOK FOR feathery-soft foliage.
BLOOM: Spring–summer

CRESTED PRICKLYPOPPY
Argemone polyanthemos
Poppy family *Papaveraceae*

ECOLOGY: Plains and foothills.

LOOK FOR a white poppy with a
yellow center on a prickly plant.

BLOOM: Summer

CROWNLEAF (CUTLEAF) EVENING PRIMROSE
Oenothera coronopifolia
Evening Primrose family *Onagraceae*

ECOLOGY: Plains to foothills in dry areas.

LOOK FOR an evening primrose having all leaves deeply cut with no uncut areas.

BLOOM: Spring–midsummer

CUTLEAF DAISY
Erigeron compositus
Aster family *Asteraceae (Compositae)*

ECOLOGY: Foothills to subalpine in dry areas.

LOOK FOR foliage similar to Rocky Mountain
  Juniper *(Juniperus scopulorum)*.

BLOOM: Summer

DIAMONDLEAF SAXIFRAGE
Saxifraga (Micranthes) rhomboidea
Saxifrage family *Saxifragaceae*

ECOLOGY: Foothills to alpine in
shade and moisture.

LOOK FOR a rosette of broad,
leathery leaves and a slender scape
bearing a cluster of tiny flowers.

BLOOM: Spring–summer

DRUMMOND'S MILKVETCH
Astragalus drummondii
Pea family *Fabaceae (Leguminosae)*

ECOLOGY: Plains to montane in open areas.

LOOK FOR a hairy leguminous plant with
  unruly, curved, white flowers.

BLOOM: Late spring–summer

DWARF (ALPINE) PHLOX
Phlox condensata
Phlox family *Polemoniaceae*

ECOLOGY: Subalpine and alpine on open slopes.

LOOK FOR green cushions with small, white flowers crowding the surface.

BLOOM: Summer

EIGHTPETAL MOUNTAIN-AVENS
Dryas octopetala
Rose family *Rosaceae*

ECOLOGY: Alpine on open slopes.

LOOK FOR a tiny, white flower with eight
  petals and leathery, toothed leaves.

BLOOM: Summer

**ELKWEED
(GREEN GENTIAN)**
Frasera speciosa
Gentian family *Gentianaceae*

ECOLOGY: Foothills to
  subalpine in moisture.

LOOK FOR an erect plant with
  lily-like leaves and whorls of
  greenish-white flowers.

BLOOM: Summer

**FEATHERY FALSE
LILY OF THE VALLEY
(FALSE SOLOMON'S SEAL)**
*Maianthemum racemosum
(Smilacina racemosa)*
Lily family *Liliaceae*

ECOLOGY: Plains to montane.

LOOK FOR two-dimensional leaf
structure and bristle-like petals.

BLOOM: Spring–summer

FENDLER'S SANDWORT
Arenaria (Eremogone) fendleri
Pink family *Caryophyllaceae*

ECOLOGY: Foothills to alpine.

LOOK FOR stripes on the calyx
and the five red anthers.

BLOOM: Summer

FIELD BINDWEED
Convolvulus arvensis
Morning Glory family *Convolvulaceae*

ECOLOGY: Plains, almost anywhere—a
  noxious weed.

LOOK FOR a twining vine with arrowhead
  leaves and funnel-shaped flowers.

BLOOM: Spring–autumn

Nonnative

FIELD CHICKWEED (MOUSE-EAR)
Cerastium arvense
Pink family *Caryophyllaceae*

ECOLOGY: Foothills and montane in open areas.

LOOK FOR a flower with cleft petals, at low elevations.

BLOOM: Spring–midsummer

FIELD PENNYCRESS
Thlaspi arvense
Mustard family *Brassicaceae (Cruciferae)*

ECOLOGY: Plains to montane.

LOOK FOR upright leaves and seed pods
with winged margins.
BLOOM: Spring–summer

FRINGED GRASS OF PARNASSUS
Parnassia fimbriata
Saxifrage family *Saxifragaceae*

ECOLOGY: Subalpine in shaded bogs.

LOOK FOR round, thick, glossy basal leaves and
  slender scapes with a single white flower.

BLOOM: Midsummer–autumn

GIANT ANGELICA
Angelica ampla
Celery (Parsley) family *Apiaceae*

ECOLOGY: Foothills to subalpine in wet places.

LOOK FOR a large flat umbel, a purpling stalk, and celery-type leaves.

BLOOM: Summer

GUNNISON'S MARIPOSA LILY
Calochortus gunnisonii
Lily family *Liliaceae*

ECOLOGY: Foothills to subalpine in
meadows and on open slopes.

LOOK FOR a bowl-shaped lily with
brown spots and a yellow center.

BLOOM: Late spring–summer

HEARTLEAF BITTERCRESS
Cardamine cordifolia
Mustard family *Brassicaceae (Cruciferae)*

ECOLOGY: Montane and subalpine.

LOOK FOR white, domed umbels on plants in or near running water.

BLOOM: Summer

HOOKER'S TOWNSEND (EASTER) DAISY
Townsendia hookeri
Aster family *Asteraceae (Compositae)*

ECOLOGY: Plains and foothills.

LOOK FOR small patches of green with several little daisy heads.

BLOOM: Spring–early summer

LANCELEAF SPRINGBEAUTY
Claytonia lanceolata (rosea)
Purslane family *Portulacaceae*

ECOLOGY: Foothills in moist areas. One of
the earliest flowers.

LOOK FOR white flowers with pink anthers.

BLOOM: Spring

LITTLELEAF (DWARF) ALUMROOT
Heuchera parvifolia nivalis
Saxifrage family *Saxifragaceae*

ECOLOGY: Montane and subalpine on rocky ledges.

LOOK FOR a basal rosette of toothed leaves and a
   grass-like flower spike.

BLOOM: Summer

MINER'S CANDLE
Cryptantha (Oreocarya) virgata
Borage family *Boraginaceae*

ECOLOGY: Foothills and
montane on dry slopes.

LOOK FOR a plant that suggests
a white candle.

BLOOM: Spring–summer

MOUNTAIN DEATHCAMAS
Zigadenus (Anticlea) elegans
Lily family *Liliaceae*

ECOLOGY: Montane to alpine in moist areas.

LOOK FOR upright basal leaves, a sturdy scape, and well-spaced flowers in a raceme.

BLOOM: Spring–summer

49

NORTHERN BEDSTRAW
Galium boreale (septentrionale)
Madder family *Rubiaceae*

ECOLOGY: Plains to subalpine in open
  woods, meadows, and on slopes.

LOOK FOR an inflorescence of
  slender axillary stalks with white
  terminal clusters.

BLOOM: Spring–summer

PARRY'S MILKVETCH
Astragalus parryi
Pea family *Fabaceae (Leguminosae)*

ECOLOGY: Montane in open areas.

LOOK FOR a curved pod. Groundplum
Milkvetch (*A. crassicarpus*) differs in
that it is found at lower elevations
and has a round pod.

BLOOM: Spring–summer

51

PEARLY (TALL) PUSSYTOES
Antennaria anaphaloides
Aster family *Asteraceae (Compositae)*

ECOLOGY: Foothills to subalpine in open, dry areas.

LOOK FOR four to seven fluffy, ball-like white
  flowers clustered atop stems 1' tall.

BLOOM: Spring–summer

RICHARDSON'S (WHITE) GERANIUM
Geranium richardsonii
Geranium family *Geraniaceae*

ECOLOGY: Foothills to subalpine in moist, shady areas.

LOOK FOR five horizontal, flat, white petals, sometimes
  having pink anthers and veins.

BLOOM: Spring–autumn

ROCKY MOUNTAIN SNOWLOVER
Chionophila jamesii
Figwort family *Scrophulariaceae*

ECOLOGY: Alpine, among rocks.

LOOK FOR white flowers that do not fully open.

BLOOM: Summer

**SCENTBOTTLE
(WHITE BOG ORCHID)**
Platanthera (Limnorchis) dilatata
Orchid family *Orchidaceae*

ECOLOGY: Montane to alpine.

LOOK FOR a spike of tiny
asymmetrical flowers.

BLOOM: Summer

**SCENTLESS FALSE MAYWEED
(WILD CHAMOMILE)**
Tripleurospermum perforatum (Matricaria, perforata)
Aster family *Asteraceae (Compositae)*

ECOLOGY: Montane and subalpine in disturbed areas.

LOOK FOR a daisy with string-like leaves.

BLOOM: Summer–autumn

Nonnative

SICKLETOP LOUSEWORT
Pedicularis racemosa
Figwort family *Scrophulariaceae*

ECOLOGY: Montane and subalpine near conifers.

LOOK FOR linear leaves up into the spike, and downward-curved corollas.

BLOOM: Summer

SINGLE DELIGHT (WOOD NYMPH)
Moneses (Pyrola) uniflora
Wintergreen family *Pyrolaceae*

ECOLOGY: Montane and subalpine.

LOOK FOR a tiny rosette of leaves with a
  nodding white flower with a green stigma.

BLOOM: Summer

SMALL-LEAF PUSSYTOES (SUNLOVING CATSPAW)

Antennaria parvifolia
Aster family *Asteraceae (Compositae)*

ECOLOGY: Foothills to subalpine on dry, sunny slopes.

LOOK FOR patches of gray-green foliage with cotton-like balls on stems less than 6" high.

BLOOM: Spring–summer

SMOOTH WHITE (PORTER) ASTER
Symphyotrichum porteri (Aster porteri)
Aster family *Asteraceae (Compositae)*

ECOLOGY: Foothills and montane.

LOOK FOR all leaves being more or less the same length.

BLOOM: Midsummer–autumn

**SOAPWEED YUCCA
(SPANISH BAYONET)**
Yucca glauca
Agave family *Agavaceae*
ECOLOGY: Plains and foothills in dry areas.
LOOK FOR sharp-pointed, bayonet-like leaves.
BLOOM: Spring–midsummer

SPIKED IPOMOPSIS
Ipomopsis spicata
Phlox family *Polemoniaceae*

ECOLOGY: Foothills.

LOOK FOR a curved stem, string-like
   leaves, and tiny, white trumpet flowers.

BLOOM: Spring–summer

STARRY FALSE LILY OF THE VALLEY (STAR SOLOMON'S SEAL)
Maianthemun (Smilacina) stellatum
Lily family *Liliaceae*

ECOLOGY: Foothills to subalpine.

LOOK FOR two-dimensional leaf structure, in-rolled, clasping leaves, and red striped fruit.

BLOOM: Spring–summer

TRAILING FLEABANE (DAISY)
Erigeron flagellaris
Aster family *Asteraceae (Compositae)*

ECOLOGY: Plains to subalpine.

LOOK FOR an upright stem with few leaves, and horizontal stems with reduced leaves.

BLOOM: Early spring–summer

TUFTED ALPINE (ROCK) SAXIFRAGE
Saxifraga caespitosa
Saxifrage family *Saxifragaceae*

ECOLOGY: Montane to alpine.

LOOK FOR moss-like patches with awl-like
leaves and little white flowers.

BLOOM: Summer

TUFTED (STEMLESS) EVENING PRIMROSE
Oenothera caespitosa
Evening Primrose family *Onagraceae*

ECOLOGY: Plains to montane in dry areas and on sunny slopes.

LOOK FOR a rosette of wavy, lanceolate leaves and a delicate, white, four-petaled flower.

BLOOM: Spring–summer

TWINFLOWER (ALPINE) SANDWORT
Minuartia (Lidia) obtusiloba
Pink family *Caryophyllaceae*

ECOLOGY: Alpine on steep slopes.

LOOK FOR moss-like leaves and white, vase-shaped
   flowers with separated petals.

BLOOM: Summer–autumn

VIRGINIA STRAWBERRY
Fragaria virginiana
Rose family *Rosaceae*

ECOLOGY: Foothills to subalpine.

LOOK FOR a strawberry plant
with prominent leaf veins.

BLOOM: Spring–summer

WESTERN PEARLY EVERLASTING
Anaphalis margaritacea
Aster family *Asteraceae (Compositae)*

ECOLOGY: Foothills to subalpine in semishade.

LOOK FOR clusters of white pearls atop erect
  stems 1' or more tall.

BLOOM: Summer–autumn

WHITE CHECKERBLOOM (CHECKERMALLOW)
Sidalcea candida
Mallow family *Malvaceae*

ECOLOGY: Subalpine in wet meadows.

LOOK FOR a flower with an exserted style and a flared stigma.

BLOOM: Summer

WHITE HAWKWEED
Hieracium albiflorum
Aster family *Asteraceae (Compositae)*

ECOLOGY: Montane.

LOOK FOR a cluster of small, white, short-rayed flowers atop a slender stalk.

BLOOM: Summer

WHITE LOCOWEED
Oxytropis sericea
Pea family *Fabaceae (Leguminosae)*

ECOLOGY: Plains to subalpine.

LOOK FOR reclining, pinnate leaves and
  racemes with ten or more flowers.

BLOOM: Spring–summer

72

WHITE MARSH MARIGOLD
Caltha (Psychrophila) leptosepala
Buttercup family *Ranunculaceae*

ECOLOGY: Subalpine and alpine in wet areas.

LOOK FOR patches of glossy leaves and white flowers with yellow centers.

BLOOM: Spring–summer

WHITISH GENTIAN
Gentiana (Gentianodes) algida
Gentian family *Gentianaceae*

ECOLOGY: Subalpine and alpine near water.

LOOK FOR tubular flowers with pointed
 lobes and purple stripes and dots.

BLOOM: Midsummer–autumn

ROCKY MOUNTAIN WILDFLOWERS

Yellow Flowers

ALPINE AVENS
Geum (Acomostylis) rossii turbinatum
Rose family *Rosaceae*

ECOLOGY: Alpine on sunny slopes.

LOOK FOR a plant having leaves with
up to twenty pairs of overlapping,
toothed leaflets and flower that is
top (turban) shaped.

BLOOM: Summer

ALPINE (SNOW) BUTTERCUP
Ranunculus adoneus (eschscholtzii adoneus)
Buttercup family *Ranunculaceae*

ECOLOGY: Subalpine and alpine in bogs.

LOOK FOR a patch of buttercups with
light green, string-like leaves and yellow
flowers with corrugated petals.

BLOOM: Summer

ALPINE FALSE SPRINGPARSLEY
Pseudocymopterus montanus
Celery family *Apiaceae (Umbelliferae)*

ECOLOGY: Subalpine and alpine.

LOOK FOR sharply incised leaves and
small yellow umbels at high elevations.

BLOOM: Spring–summer

ARROWLEAF RAGWORT (SENECIO)
Senecio triangularis
Aster family *Asteraceae (Compositae)*

ECOLOGY: Subalpine in moist forests.

LOOK FOR arrowhead leaves with toothed
  margins.

BLOOM: Summer

BIGFLOWER (LEAFY) CINQUEFOIL
Potentilla (Drymocallis) fissa
Rose family *Rosaceae*

ECOLOGY: Foothills to subalpine.

LOOK FOR a cinquefoil with an abundance of broad,
   bright green leaflets and pale yellow flowers.

BLOOM: Late spring–summer

BIRD'S-FOOT TREFOIL (DEERVETCH)
Lotus corniculatus
Pea family *Fabaceae (Leguminosae)*

ECOLOGY: Plains and foothills.

LOOK FOR bright, yellow flowers on a plant that resembles alfalfa.

BLOOM: Midsummer

BLACKEYED SUSAN
Rudbeckia hirta
Aster family *Asteraceae (Compositae)*

ECOLOGY: Foothills to montane.

LOOK FOR dark brown, domed discs.

BLOOM: Summer

BROOMLIKE RAGWORT (BROOM SENECIO)
Senecio spartioides
Aster family *Asteraceae (Compositae)*

ECOLOGY: Plains and foothills.

LOOK FOR grass-like leaves alternately arranged, unreduced, up to the top.

BLOOM: Midsummer–autumn

BUTTER AND EGGS
Linaria vulgaris
Figwort family *Scrophulariaceae*

ECOLOGY: Plains to subalpine in disturbed areas—a noxious weed.

LOOK FOR yellow, spurred flowers and linear leaves on a stiff, unbranched stem.

BLOOM: Spring–summer

Nonnative

**COMMON GAILLARDIA
(BLANKET FLOWER)**
Gaillardia aristata
Aster family *Asteraceae (Compositae)*

ECOLOGY: Plains to montane.

LOOK FOR a large reddish disc
  surrounded by yellow rays.

BLOOM: Summer

COMMON SUNFLOWER
Helianthus annuus
Aster family *Asteraceae (Compositae)*

ECOLOGY: Plains, along roadsides.

LOOK FOR a tall plant with a large,
nodding, terminal flower.

BLOOM: Summer–autumn

CREEPING BARBERRY (HOLLYGRAPE)
Mahonia repens
Barberry family *Berberidaceae*

ECOLOGY: Foothills and montane on hillsides, often in association with conifers and oaks.

LOOK FOR evergreen leaves that have a papery texture.

BLOOM: Spring–midsummer

CUTLEAF (TALL) CONEFLOWER
Rudbeckia laciniata (ampla)
Aster family *Asteraceae (Compositae)*

ECOLOGY: Foothills to montane in wet,
shady places.

LOOK FOR a domed receptacle and five
to fifteen rays on a 3" yellow flower.

BLOOM: Summer

DALMATION TOADFLAX
Linaria dalmatica
Figwort family *Scrophulariaceae*

ECOLOGY: Plains and foothills in disturbed areas—a noxious weed.

LOOK FOR yellow flowers with a long spur and orange flower buds.

BLOOM: Spring–aututmn

Nonnative

DWARF MOUNTAIN (ROCK) RAGWORT
Senecio fremontii
Aster family *Asteraceae (Compositae)*

ECOLOGY: Subalpine and alpine.

LOOK FOR glossy, thick leaves with sharp pointed teeth on a dwarf, compact plant.

BLOOM: Summer

FENDLER'S (GROUNDSEL) RAGWORT
Packera (Senecio) fendleri
Aster family *Asteraceae (Compositae)*
ECOLOGY: Foothills and montane in clearings.
LOOK FOR leaves with blunt teeth.
BLOOM: Midsummer–autumn

**FIVENERVE HELIANTHELLA
(NODDING SUNFLOWER)**
Helianthella quinquenervis
Aster family *Asteraceae (Compositae)*

ECOLOGY: Montane to subalpine.

LOOK FOR narrow, opposite, glossy
 leaves and a 3" sunflower.

BLOOM: Summer

FOOTHILL ARNICA
Arnica fulgens
Aster family *Asteraceae (Compositae)*

ECOLOGY: Foothills to alpine.

LOOK FOR a solitary, daisy-like flower and hairy, paired stem leaves.

BLOOM: Spring–summer

**FRONT RANGE TWINPOD
(DOUBLE BLADDER POD)**
Physaria bellii
Mustard family *Brassicaceae (Cruciferae)*

ECOLOGY: Foothills and montane.

LOOK FOR a rosette of gray-green leaves,
ascending stems, and yellow clusters of
four-petaled flowers.

BLOOM: Spring

94

GOLDEN DRABA
Draba aurea
Mustard family *Brassicaceae (Cruciferae)*

ECOLOGY: Montane to alpine.

LOOK FOR twisted pods—they are diagnostic.

BLOOM: Summer

**GRAYLOCKS FOUR-NERVE DAISY
(ALPINE SUNFLOWER)**
Tetraneuris (Hymenoxys) grandiflora
Aster family *Asteraceae (Compositae)*

ECOLOGY: Alpine slopes among rocks.

LOOK FOR string-like leaves and a proportionally
  large flower with a domed center.

BLOOM: Summer

HAIRY EVENING PRIMROSE
Oenothera villosa
Evening Primrose family *Onagraceae*

ECOLOGY: Plains to montane on hillsides.

LOOK FOR ascending, leafy stems and
  yellow flowers arising from leaf axils.

BLOOM: Early summer–autumn

HEARTLEAF ARNICA
Arnica cordifolia
Aster family *Asteraceae (Compositae)*

ECOLOGY: Foothills to alpine in the
  shade of conifers.

LOOK FOR heart-shaped leaves.

BLOOM: Spring–summer

HOARY (WERNER'S) GROUNDSEL
Packera (Senecio) werneriifolia
Aster family *Asteraceae (Compositae)*

ECOLOGY: Subalpine and alpine on rocky ridges.

LOOK FOR a small clump of upright, hairy, gray-green leaves and yellow flowers with spaced rays.

BLOOM: Summer–autumn

LAMBSTONGUE (GROUNDSEL) RAGWORT
Senecio integerrimus
Aster family *Asteraceae (Compositae)*

ECOLOGY: Foothills to subalpine in dry sites.

LOOK FOR ascending, wavy leaves and an erect, sparsely
leafed stem with ten to fifteen flower heads.

BLOOM: Spring–midsummer

LITTLE (BUSH) SUNFLOWER
Helianthus pumilus
Aster family *Asteraceae (Compositae)*

ECOLOGY: Foothills and montane.

LOOK FOR gray-green, hairy, lanceolate
  leaves that are unusually uniform.

BLOOM: Summer

MISSOURI (SMOOTH) GOLDENROD
Solidago missouriensis
Aster family *Asteraceae (Compositae)*

ECOLOGY: Plains to montane on rocky slopes and in forest openings.

LOOK FOR alternate, linear leaves extending up to the inflorescence.

BLOOM: Midsummer–autumn

MULE-EARS
Wyethia amplexicaulis
Aster family *Asteraceae (Compositae)*

ECOLOGY: Foothills and montane forming
  colorful patches on open areas.

LOOK FOR patches of bright yellow flowers
  along roadways.

BLOOM: Spring–summer

NARROWLEAF (PUCCOON) STONESEED
Lithospermum incisum
Borage family *Boraginaceae*

ECOLOGY: Plains and foothills in open dry areas.

LOOK FOR succulent, linear leaves and trumpet-like flowers.

BLOOM: Spring–midsummer

NUTTALL'S (YELLOW) VIOLET
Viola nuttallii
Violet family *Violaceae*

ECOLOGY: Plains to subalpine.

LOOK FOR a tiny yellow violet with
 brown streaks on the lowest petal.

BLOOM: Spring–midsummer

PLANTAINLEAF (CALTHA FLOWERED) BUTTERCUP
Ranunculus alismifolius (alismaefolius)
Buttercup family *Ranunculaceae*

ECOLOGY: Subalpine and alpine in bogs.

LOOK FOR a Marsh Marigold *(Caltha leptosepala)* with yellow flowers.

BLOOM: Spring–summer

PRAIRIE FALSE (WAVYLEAF) DANDELION
Nothocalais cuspidata
Aster family *Asteraceae (Compositae)*

ECOLOGY: Plains and foothills.

LOOK FOR leaves with whitish margins and midribs.

BLOOM: Spring–early summer

**SCRAMBLED EGGS
(GOLDEN CORYDALIS)**
Corydalis aurea
Fumitory family *Fumariaceae*

ECOLOGY: Foothills and montane.

LOOK FOR a small plant with parsley-like
leaves and yellow, spurred flowers.

BLOOM: Spring–autumn

SEEP (YELLOW) MONKEYFLOWER
Mimulus guttatus
Figwort family *Scrophulariaceae*

ECOLOGY: Montane and subalpine in moist areas.

LOOK FOR opposite, clasping leaves and a yellow, five-lobed, tubular flower.

BLOOM: Spring–summer

SPEARLEAF STONECROP
Sedum (Amerosedum) lanceolatum
Stonecrop family *Crassulaceae*

ECOLOGY: Plains to alpine.

LOOK FOR moss-like rosettes, red
stems, and terminal clusters of
three to six yellow flowers.

BLOOM: Summer

SPREADFRUIT GOLDENBANNER
Thermopsis divaricarpa (rhombifolia)
Pea family *Fabaceae (Leguminosae)*

ECOLOGY: Foothills to subalpine.

LOOK FOR a single stem with trifoliate
   leaves and an upright raceme of bright
   yellow flowers.

BLOOM: Spring–midsummer

SUBALPINE GUMWEED
Grindelia subalpina
Aster family *Asteraceae (Compositae)*

ECOLOGY: Montane to subalpine.

LOOK FOR gummy bracts and wavy
  upper stem leaves.

BLOOM: Summer–autumn

SULPHUR-FLOWER (SUBALPINE) BUCKWHEAT
Eriogonum umbellatum (subalpinum) majus
Buckwheat family *Polygonaceae*

ECOLOGY: Montane to alpine.

LOOK FOR ten to twenty small white umbels forming a
head subtended by a whorl of leaves.

BLOOM: Summer

TALL BLACKTIP RAGWORT (BLACK-TIPPED SENECIO)

Senecio atratus
Aster family *Asteraceae (Compositae)*

ECOLOGY: Montane to alpine in scree and rock slides.

LOOK FOR brown tips on the bracts under the flower heads.

BLOOM: Summer

TENPETAL BLAZINGSTAR
Mentzelia decapetala
Loasa family *Loasaceae*

ECOLOGY: Montane on rocky hillsides.

LOOK FOR the unique saw-tooth leaves
and yellow flowers with ten petals.

BLOOM: Midsummer–autumn

TWISTSPINE PRICKLYPEAR
Opuntia macrorhiza
Cactus family *Cactaceae*

ECOLOGY: Plains and foothills in dry areas.

LOOK FOR a spiny, green, oval, upright
   pad with one or more rose-like flowers.

BLOOM: Late spring–summer

**UPRIGHT PRAIRIE CONEFLOWER
(MEXICAN HAT)**
Ratibida columnifera
Aster family *Asteraceae (Compositae)*

ECOLOGY: Plains and foothills.

LOOK FOR the column of disc flowers and
the whorl of rays that form a hat.

BLOOM: Summer

WESTERN (YELLOW) INDIAN PAINTBRUSH
Castilleja occidentalis
Figwort family *Scrophulariaceae*

ECOLOGY: Subalpine and alpine in open areas.

LOOK FOR overlapping yellow bracts and stemless leaves.

BLOOM: Late spring–summer

WESTERN WALLFLOWER
Erysimum asperum
Mustard family *Brassicaceae (Cruciferae)*

ECOLOGY: Foothills to subalpine in open areas.

LOOK FOR leaves and pods extending out from
the stem. This distinguishes it from Sandune
Wallflower *(E. capitatum)*.

BLOOM: Spring–summer

WHISKBROOM PARSLEY
Harbouria trachypleura
Celery family *Apiaceae (Umbelliferae)*

ECOLOGY: Foothills and montane.

LOOK FOR string-like foliage and an umbel
composed of several smaller umbels.

BLOOM: Spring–early summer

YELLOW AVALANCHE-LILY
Erythronium grandiflorum
Lily family *Liliaceae*

ECOLOGY: Montane to alpine in bogs.

LOOK FOR a leafless stalk bearing a
single, yellow, nodding lily.

BLOOM: Spring–summer

YELLOW OWL'S CLOVER
Orthocarpus luteus
Figwort family *Scrophulariaceae*

ECOLOGY: Montane in exposed areas.

LOOK FOR a leafy raceme with yellow
   tubular flowers and linear leaves.

BLOOM: Summer

YELLOW SALSIFY
Tragopogon dubius
Aster family *Asteraceae (Compositae)*

ECOLOGY: Plains to montane in waste areas.

LOOK FOR narrow, upright, clasping, sharply
   pointed, grass-like leaves and yellow
   flower heads with needle-like bracts.

BLOOM: Late spring–midsummer

YELLOW SWEETCLOVER
Melilotus officinalis
Pea family *Fabaceae (Leguminosae)*

ECOLOGY: Plains to montane—a noxious weed.

LOOK FOR a tall plant with trifoliate leaves and racemes of yellow, drooping flowers.

BLOOM: Summer

Nonnative

ROCKY MOUNTAIN WILDFLOWERS

Red
Flowers

ALPINE (MOUNTAIN) LAUREL
Kalmia microphylla
Heath family *Ericaceae*

ECOLOGY: Subalpine and alpine in moisture.

LOOK FOR pink flowers with exserted styles
  and stamens.

BLOOM: Midsummer

ALPINE LEWISIA (PYGMY BITTERROOT)
Lewisia (Oreobroma) pygmaea
Purslane family *Portulacaceae*

ECOLOGY: Subalpine and alpine in moisture.

LOOK FOR a tiny rosette of narrow, upright leaves and a saucer-shaped flower.

BLOOM: Summer

ALPINE PRIMROSE
Primula angustifolia
Primrose family *Primulaceae*

ECOLOGY: Alpine slopes, in colonies, among rocks.

LOOK FOR a tiny pink primrose at high elevations.

BLOOM: Summer

DARKTHROAT SHOOTINGSTAR
Dodecatheon pulchellum
Primrose family *Primulaceae*

ECOLOGY: Foothills to subalpine in cool, shady, wet places.

LOOK FOR a pink flower with swept-back petals and protruding stamens.

BLOOM: Spring–midsummer

**DOTTED BLAZING STAR
(GAY FEATHER)**
Liatris punctata
Aster family *Asteraceae (Compositae)*

ECOLOGY: Plains and foothills.

LOOK FOR a spike of feathery flowers that
open from the top of the spike on down.

BLOOM: Midsummer–autumn

ELEPHANTHEAD LOUSEWORT
Pedicularis groenlandica
Figwort family *Scrophulariaceae*

ECOLOGY: Montane to alpine in moisture.

LOOK FOR pink elephant heads.

BLOOM: Summer

FAIRY SLIPPER
Calypso bulbosa
Orchid family *Orchidaceae*

ECOLOGY: Foothills to subalpine in deep, moist
forests—a beautiful and endangered species.

LOOK FOR the unmistakable pink slipper.

BLOOM: Late spring–midsummer

FIREWEED
Chamerion (Epilobium) angustifolium
Evening Primrose family *Onagraceae*

ECOLOGY: Foothills to subalpine.

LOOK FOR pink flowers with exserted
styles in loosely flowered racemes.

BLOOM: Summer–autumn

GIANT RED INDIAN (SCARLET) PAINTBRUSH
Castilleja miniata
Figwort family *Scrophulariaceae*

ECOLOGY: Foothills to subalpine.

LOOK FOR dense spikes of bright red bracts.

BLOOM: Summer

LEDGE STONECROP (KING'S CROWN)
Rhodiola (Sedum) integrifolia
Stonecrop family *Crassulaceae*

ECOLOGY: Subalpine and alpine in moisture.

LOOK FOR a short, succulent plant with a dark red terminal umbel.

BLOOM: Summer

LIVERLEAF (BOG) WINTERGREEN
Pyrola asarifolia (rotundifolia)
Wintergreen family *Pyrolaceae*

ECOLOGY: Montane and subalpine in moisture.

LOOK FOR a rosette of glossy leaves and a
   raceme of pink, nodding, global flowers.

BLOOM: Summer

MOSS CAMPION
Silene acaulis
Pink family *Caryophyllaceae*

ECOLOGY: Alpine, on exposed slopes.

LOOK FOR five-lobed pink flowers
springing up from what appears to
be a patch of bright green turf.

BLOOM: Summer

NODDING ONION
Allium cernuum
Lily family *Liliaceae*

ECOLOGY: Foothills to subalpine on grassy slopes.

LOOK FOR nodding, pink onion flowers.

BLOOM: Summer

PARRY'S CLOVER
Trifolium parryi
Pea family *Fabaceae (Leguminosae)*

ECOLOGY: Subalpine and alpine in moisture.

LOOK FOR a pink flower head with eight to twelve leguminous flowers on a short scape.

BLOOM: Summer

PARRY'S PRIMROSE
Primula parryi
Primrose family *Primulaceae*

ECOLOGY: Subalpine and alpine in or near moving water.

LOOK FOR panicles of beautiful rose-colored flowers near or in running water.

BLOOM: Summer

PINEYWOODS GERANIUM
Geranium caespitosum
Geranium family *Geraniaceae*

ECOLOGY: Foothills to subalpine.

LOOK FOR pink, saucer-shaped
flowers, five overlapping
petals, and exserted styles.

BLOOM: Spring–autumn

141

PIPSISSEWA
Chimaphila umbellata
Wintergreen family *Pyrolaceae*

ECOLOGY: Foothills and montane
in moisture, under conifers.

LOOK FOR pink or white flowers,
berry-like buds, and glossy,
evergreen leaves.

BLOOM: Summer

PURPLE (VIOLET) PRAIRIE CLOVER
Dalea purpurea
Pea family *Fabaceae (Leguminosae)*

ECOLOGY: Foothills on dry hillsides.

LOOK FOR straight, yellowish stems, linear
leaflets, and pink flowers with exserted
styles and stamens.

BLOOM: Summer

**REDPOD STONECROP
(QUEEN'S CROWN)**
Rhodiola (Sedum, Clementsia) rhodantha
Stonecrop family *Crassulaceae*

ECOLOGY: Subalpine and alpine in moisture.

LOOK FOR stems with many succulent leaves
and rose-colored umbels.

BLOOM: Summer

ROSY (PINK) PUSSYTOES
Antennaria rosea
Aster family *Asteraceae (Compositae)*

ECOLOGY: Foothills to alpine.

LOOK FOR a tiny wooly plant with
  several pink flower heads resembling
  a kitten's toes.

BLOOM: Summer

SCARLET (GUARA) BEEBLOSSOM
Gaura coccinea
Evening Primrose family *Onagraceae*

ECOLOGY: Plains to montane.

LOOK FOR red, pink, and white flowers as
they pass from bud to flower to senescence.

BLOOM: Spring–midsummer

SCARLET GILIA
Ipomopsis aggregata
Phlox family *Polemoniaceae*
ECOLOGY: Foothills and montane.
LOOK FOR bright red trumpet flowers.
BLOOM: Summer–autumn

SCARLET GLOBEMALLOW (COPPER MALLOW)
Sphaeralcea coccinea
Mallow family *Malvaceae*

ECOLOGY: Plains and foothills.

LOOK FOR a five-petaled orange flower and deeply incised leaves.

BLOOM: Early summer–autumn

SHOWY MILKWEED
Asclepias speciosa
Milkweed family *Asclepiadaceae*

ECOLOGY: Plains and foothills near water.

LOOK FOR a pink cluster of star-shaped
flowers, shiny leaves, and milky sap.

BLOOM: Summer

SUMMER (SPOTTED) CORALROOT
Corallorrhiza maculata
Orchid family *Orchidaceae*

ECOLOGY: Foothills to subalpine in decaying
   duff of conifers.

LOOK FOR red, succulent stems bearing little
   orchids with purple dots on the lower lobe.

BLOOM: Late spring–summer

TWINFLOWER
Linnaea borealis
Honeysuckle family *Caprifoliaceae*

ECOLOGY: Montane to subalpine.
Named for renowned botanist
Carolus Linnaeus.

LOOK FOR little flowers hanging like
twin lanterns on a lamp pole.

BLOOM: Summer

WESTERN RED COLUMBINE
Aquilegia elegantula
Buttercup family *Ranunculaceae*

ECOLOGY: Montane and subalpine
 in shade.

LOOK FOR five red, trailing spurs.

BLOOM: Summer

WOOD LILY
Lilium philadelphicum
Lily family *Liliaceae*

ECOLOGY: Foothills and montane in moisture—a beautiful, rare, and endangered species.

LOOK FOR a 4" lily; there is only one.

BLOOM: Midsummer

WOODLAND PINEDROPS
Pterospora andromedea
Pinesap family *Monotopaceae*

ECOLOGY: Foothills and montane—associated with pine forests, in deep shade.

LOOK FOR a reddish asparagus-like stalk and orange bead-like flowers on a raceme.

BLOOM: Summer

WOODS' (WILD) ROSE
Rosa woodsii
Rose family *Rosaceae*

ECOLOGY: Plains to subalpine in sun.

LOOK FOR a rose with a single set of petals and a large yellow center.

BLOOM: Summer

WYOMING INDIAN PAINTBRUSH
Castilleja linariifolia
Figwort family *Scrophulariaceae*

ECOLOGY: Foothills to montane; the state flower of Wyoming.

LOOK FOR a red paintbrush with a loose spike and prominent axillary branches.

BLOOM: Summer

ROCKY MOUNTAIN WILDFLOWERS

Blue
Flowers

AMERICAN ALPINE SPEEDWELL
Veronica wormskjoldii (nutans)
Figwort family *Scrophulariaceae*

ECOLOGY: Subalpine and alpine in moisture.

LOOK FOR stems with opposite, uniformly sized leaves and a tight terminal flower cluster.

BLOOM: Midsummer

ARCTIC ALPINE FORGET-ME-NOT
Eritrichium nanum
Borage family *Boraginaceae*

ECOLOGY: Alpine slopes in colonies among rocks.

LOOK FOR tiny blue flowers at high elevations.

BLOOM: Summer

AUTUMN DWARF (NORTHERN) GENTIAN
Gentianella amarella
Gentian family *Gentianaceae*

ECOLOGY: Subalpine and alpine in moisture.

LOOK FOR purple or pink barrel-shaped flowers with
   five lobes. Expect wide variation in this species.

BLOOM: Midsummer–autumn

BLUEBELL BELLFLOWER (COMMON HAREBELL)
Campanula rotundifolia
Bellflower family *Campanulaceae*

ECOLOGY: Foothills to alpine.

LOOK FOR nodding, blue, bell-shaped flowers on slender plants.

BLOOM: Summer

BRITTON'S SKULLCAP
Scutellaria brittonii
Mint family *Lamiaceae (Labiatae)*

ECOLOGY: Plains and foothills.

LOOK FOR a beaked flower with a patch of white on the lower lip.

BLOOM: Spring–early summer

COLORADO BLUE COLUMBINE
Aquilegia coerulea
Buttercup family *Ranunculaceae*

ECOLOGY: Foothills to alpine in moisture—Colorado's state flower.

LOOK FOR the classic Columbine flower.

BLOOM: Summer

COLUMBIAN MONKSHOOD
Aconitum columbianum
Buttercup family *Ranunculaceae*

ECOLOGY: Montane to alpine in moisture.

LOOK FOR a monk's hood flower that is about the right size to wear on the little finger.

BLOOM: Midsummer–autumn

CROSSFLOWER (BLUE MUSTARD)
Chorispora tenella
Mustard family *Brassicaceae (Cruciferae)*

ECOLOGY: Plains, in open places.

LOOK FOR flower lobes that are pinched inward at the base—a diagnostic trait.

BLOOM: Spring–midsummer

DAMES ROCKET
Hesperis matronalis
Mustard family *Brassicaceae (Cruciferae)*

ECOLOGY: Plains and foothills near water.

LOOK FOR tall, slender plants with racemes of pink flowers.

BLOOM: Spring–early summer

Nonnative

EASTERN (AMERICAN) PASQUEFLOWER
Pulsatilla patens
Buttercup family *Ranunculaceae*

ECOLOGY: Foothills and montane.

LOOK FOR string-like leaves, a bowl-shaped terminal flower, or a seed-bearing, fuzzy ball.

BLOOM: Early spring

FELWORT (STAR GENTIAN)
Swertia perennis
Gentian family *Gentianaceae*

ECOLOGY: Montane to alpine in moisture.

LOOK FOR a rosette of glossy leaves, purple
  stems, and five-petaled, star-like flowers.

BLOOM: Midsummer–autumn

HAIRY CLEMATIS (SUGAR BOWL)
Clematis hirsutissima
Buttercup family *Ranunculaceae*

ECOLOGY: Foothills to montane.

LOOK FOR a large, solitary, bell-shaped
   flower and opposite leaves dissected
   into string-like segments.

BLOOM: Spring–midsummer

**HOOKEDSPUR VIOLET
(MOUNTAIN BLUE VIOLET)**
Viola adunca
Violet family *Violaceae*

ECOLOGY: Montane to alpine in meadows.

LOOK FOR a light blue violet with a spurred lower petal.

BLOOM: Spring–summer

JACOB'S LADDER
Polemonium pulcherrimum
Phlox family *Polemoniaceae*

ECOLOGY: Subalpine and alpine in shade.

LOOK FOR the ladder-like arrangement of
   the leaflets on the midrib.

BLOOM: Summer

LEWIS (PRAIRIE, BLUE) FLAX
Linum (Adenolinum) lewisii
Flax family *Linaceae*

ECOLOGY: Plains to montane.

LOOK FOR a blue, saucer-shaped flower
  with five blue petals on a slender plant.

BLOOM: Spring–summer

**MANYFLOWER STICKSEED
(FALSE FORGET-ME-NOT)**
Hackelia floribunda
Borage family *Boraginaceae*

ECOLOGY: Foothills to subalpine.

LOOK FOR axillary shoots emerging at
forty-five-degree angle and bearing
clusters of tiny blue flowers.

BLOOM: Summer

PARRY'S (PURPLE) BELLFLOWER
Campanula parryi
Bellflower family *Campanulaceae*

ECOLOGY: Foothills to subalpine in moisture.

LOOK FOR a solitary, terminal, five-lobed,
bell-shaped flower on a slender stem.

BLOOM: Summer

PARRY'S (MOUNTAIN) GENTIAN
Gentiana (Pneumonanthe) parryi
Gentian family *Gentianaceae*

ECOLOGY: Montane to alpine in moisture.

LOOK FOR a Gentian at high elevations with a five-lobed blue flower and broad, opposite leaves.

BLOOM: Midsummer–autumn

PERENNIAL FRINGED (TWISTED) GENTIAN
Gentianopsis barbellata
Gentian family *Gentianaceae*

ECOLOGY: Subalpine and alpine.

LOOK FOR a tiny plant with narrow, fleshy leaves and a solitary terminal flower with four lavender lobes.

BLOOM: Summer

PRAIRIE (WESTERN) SPIDERWORT
Tradescantia occidentalis
Spiderwort family *Commelinaceae*

ECOLOGY: Plains and foothills.

LOOK FOR a grass-like plant with blue, three-petaled flowers.

BLOOM: Spring–midsummer

PURPLE (COLORADO) LOCOWEED
Oxytropis lambertii
Pea family *Fabaceae (Leguminosae)*

ECOLOGY: Plains and foothills.

LOOK FOR a white-striped patch on a pink leguminous flower.

BLOOM: Spring–summer

ROCKY MOUNTAIN BEEPLANT
Cleome serrulata
Caper family *Capparaceae*

ECOLOGY: Plains in moist places.

LOOK FOR pink umbels that progress
upward with plant growth.

BLOOM: Summer

ROCKY MOUNTAIN (WILD) IRIS
Iris missouriensis
Iris family *Iridaceae*

ECOLOGY: Foothills to subalpine in moisture.

LOOK FOR three drooping petals and three
  upright petals, all blue.

BLOOM: Spring–midsummer

ROCKY MOUNTAIN (WHITE) PHLOX
Phlox multiflora
Phlox family *Polemoniaceae*

ECOLOGY: Foothills in dry areas.

LOOK FOR a small purplish-white flower with
grass-like leaves.

BLOOM: Spring–early summer

RYDBERG'S PENSTEMON
Penstemon rydbergii
Figwort family *Scrophulariaceae*

ECOLOGY: Montane to alpine.

LOOK FOR a Penstemon with narrow, in-folded, bright green leaves and ascending stems.

BLOOM: Summer

SILKY PHACELIA (PURPLE FRINGE)
Phacelia sericea
Waterleaf family *Hydrophyllaceae*

ECOLOGY: Montane to alpine.

LOOK FOR deeply lobed, pinnatifid leaves
  and purple or pink pincushion-like clusters.

BLOOM: Summer

SILVERY LUPINE
Lupinus argenteus
Pea family *Fabaceae (Leguminosae)*

ECOLOGY: Foothills to subalpine.

LOOK FOR leaves with five to nine
finger-like leaflets and a raceme of
leguminous flowers.

BLOOM: Early summer–autumn

STICKY POLEMONIUM (SKY PILOT)
Polemonium viscosum
Phlox family *Polemoniaceae*

ECOLOGY: Subalpine and alpine.

LOOK FOR clusters of fifteen to twenty blue
   flowers on an 8" stalk.

BLOOM: Summer

STRICT BLUE-EYED GRASS
Sisyrinchium montanum
Iris family *Iridaceae*

ECOLOGY: Foothills to subalpine.

LOOK FOR a grass-like plant with blue
   flowers borne about 2" below the tip
   of the plant.

BLOOM: Spring–midsummer

SWAMP VERBENA (BLUE VERVAIN)
Verbena hastata
Vervain family *Verbenaceae*

ECOLOGY: Plains and foothills near water—a
  noxious weed.

LOOK FOR clusters of terminal spikes with
  whorls of pink flowers progressing upward.

BLOOM: Summer

TALL (CHIMING) FRINGED BLUEBELLS
Mertensia ciliata
Borage family *Boraginaceae*

ECOLOGY: Montane to alpine in moisture.

LOOK FOR a tall *Mertensia* with nodding
terminal clusters on axillary branches.

BLOOM: Summer

TANSYLEAF TANSYASTER
Machaeranthera tanacetifolia
Aster family *Asteraceae (Compositae)*

ECOLOGY: Plains on dry land.

LOOK FOR flowers with hooked phyllaries
  and leaves with spaced, linear lobes.

BLOOM: Summer–autumn

TUFTED FLEABANE
Erigeron caespitosus
Aster family *Asteraceae (Compositae)*

ECOLOGY: Foothills in open areas.

LOOK FOR a small, lavender daisy with
hair-like petals and wavy leaves.

BLOOM: Summer–autumn

**WHIPPLE'S PENSTEMON
(DUSKY BEARDS TONGUE)**
Penstemon whippleanus
Figwort family *Scrophulariaceae*

ECOLOGY: Subalpine to alpine.

LOOK FOR corrugated corollas.

BLOOM: Summer

WILD BERGAMOT (HORSEMINT)
Monarda fistulosa
Mint family *Lamiaceae (Labiatae)*

ECOLOGY: Plains to montane in the open.

LOOK FOR opposite leaves and a terminal
   cluster of pink flowers.

BLOOM: Summer

ABOUT THE AUTHORS

Photographer **Marlene Borneman** spends much of her free time in the field locating and photographing wildflowers in their native habitats. She has studied and photographed Colorado flora since 1974. An avid hiker, she soon developed a deep interest in wildflowers as she gained knowledge of the fascinating world of identifying and capturing them in photos. She is a member of the Colorado Native Plant Society. The key to her success in photographing plants is patience and practice, as well as an understanding of the best early morning or late afternoon light to capture the brilliant colors of the wildflowers of the Rocky Mountains. It is her hope that *Rocky Mountain Wildflowers* encourages others to explore the world of Colorado flora.

James Ells, Ph.D., had an academic career for 35 years that included teaching, extension, and research in horticulture at Colorado State University in Fort Collins. After collecting his own photographs of wildflowers encountered on his hikes, he decided to write a guidebook so that anyone could use the information to identify any common plant in the field. His work culminated in *Rocky Mountain Flora*, published in its second edition by The Colorado Mountain Club Press in 2011. The identifications in *Rocky Mountain Wildflowers* follow his observations, and use the naming conventions standardized by the USDA in its database (USDA, NRCS. 2012. The PLANTS Database [http://plants.usda.gov, 2012]. National Plant Data Team, Greensboro, NC 27401-4901 USA).

INDEX OF LATIN NAMES

**For more extensive information
about the world of plants found
in the Rocky Mountain region, read
Rocky Mountain Flora, Second Edition**

by JAMES ELLS, Ph.D.

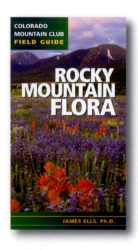

A colorful and comprehensive master reference, *Rocky Mountain Flora* provides descriptive details that characterize each plant, including comments on the stems, leaves, flowers, fruit, and seeds of the multitude of flora species that populate the Rocky Mountains.

This field guide is organized by color and also provides sections on grasses, sedges, rushes, mushrooms, ferns and fern-like plants, lichens, and edible native plants, plus a self-contained "Life List" for serious wildflower enthusiasts.

ISBN 978-0-9842213-4-9

$24.95

Published by The Colorado Mountain Club Press